Mysterious Monsters

By Michael Sandler

Scott Foresman
is an imprint of

Glenview, Illinois • Boston, Massachusetts • Chandler, Arizona •
Upper Saddle River, New Jersey

Photographs
Every effort has been made to secure permission and provide appropriate credit for photographic material. The publisher deeply regrets any omission and pledges to correct errors called to its attention in subsequent editions.

Unless otherwise acknowledged, all photographs are the property of Pearson Education, Inc.

Photo locators denoted as follows: Top (T), Center (C), Bottom (B), Left (L), Right (R), Background (Bkgd)

Cover Sam Forencich/Corbis; **1** Paul Souders/Riser/Getty Images; **3** (R) Interfoto Pressebildagentur/Alamy Images; **4** Getty Images; **5** Keystone/Getty Images; **7** Dung Vo Trung/Corbis; **8** Krause, Johansen/Getty Images; **9** Paul Souders/Riser/Getty Images; **10** Fortean/Topham/The Image Works, Inc.; **11** Bettman/Corbis; **12** Jeff Meldrum/Idaho State University; **13** Peter Anderson/©DK Images; **14** Dave Rubert Photography; **15** Tim Biscardi; **16** Tim Biscardi; **18** Malcolm Chandler/©DK Images; **19** ©The Granger Collection, NY; **20** Alamy Images; **21** Dale O'Dell/Alamy Images; **23** Reinhard Dirscherl/ Photolibrary Group, Inc.

ISBN 13: 978-0-328-51657-5
ISBN 10:   0-328-51657-0

4 5 6 7 8 9 10 V0FL 14 13 12 11

Introduction

You may have heard stories about unusual monsters. Some of the most common stories are about giant sea monsters that are strong enough to sink ships, apelike beasts that walk upright on two feet, fierce snow creatures that haunt the high mountains, or dinosaurlike serpents that swim deep within faraway lakes. These monsters have names that you may have heard too: The Giant Squid, Bigfoot, the Abominable Snowman, and the Loch Ness Monster.

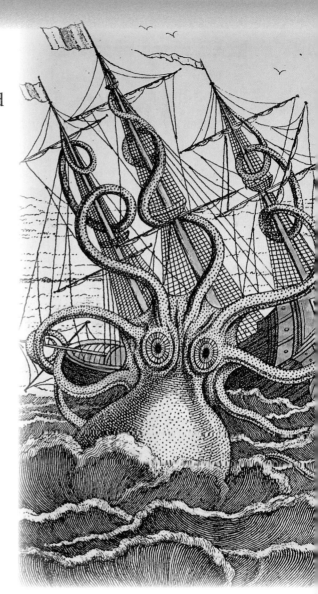

Many people claim to have seen them. But do they really exist? What do they have in common? Let's take a closer look. We'll see what the scientists say and **identify** the truth about these mysterious monsters.

Loch Ness Monster

One of the world's most famous monsters is named the Loch Ness Monster, although she more commonly is referred to by the nickname "Nessie." As the stories tell, she lurks beneath the surface of Scotland's Loch Ness. This large lake is about 23 miles long and 800 feet deep—that's plenty of dark water for a monster to hide in!

Nessie's story isn't a new one. The first tales of monster sightings in Loch Ness's waters date back some 1,500 years. For centuries, however, few people heard them. The lake was difficult to reach, and few people ventured out to visit it. Then, in the 1930s, a road was built that led to the shores of the lake. More people drove by. More people claimed to see the monster.

Stories about Nessie began in Scotland and spread all around the world. A big story ran in newspapers in 1934. A man named Robert Wilson was driving past the lake. The water started moving, rolling, and surging wildly. A friend of Wilson's shouted, "It's the monster!" Wilson snapped a photo. It soon became famous.

Wilson's photo seemed to show a swimming water creature with a long neck, pointy-head, and humped back. It looked a lot like a *plesiosaur*, a dinosaur thought to have died out millions of years ago.

Since 1934, many more people claimed to have seen Nessie. And each year, thousands of people travel to Scotland just to visit Loch Ness in hopes of sighting Nessie. The huge groups of tourists have brought a lot of business to area shops, hotels, and restaurants. These businesses then use the money to provide more comforts for future tourists.

In addition to monster-hunters, the lake draws scientists, as well. Many teams of researchers have traveled to the lake to try to find the monster. So far, none of them have had any luck.

In 2003, British scientists decided to settle the question once and for all. Does Nessie exist? They brought high-tech tools: radar and satellite technology. Using them, the team carried out a **relentless analysis** of the bottom of the lake.

What did they find? Nothing. No monster. No dinosaur. No Nessie. If Nessie doesn't exist, what have people been seeing? Can hundreds of people all be wrong? Scientists have several explanations.

What people think are dinosaurs may be otters, fish, or even **hollow** logs. If people have it in their minds that a monster is in the water, it's easy for their eyes to play tricks on them. To prove this, scientists hid an ordinary fence post in the water beneath Loch Ness. A group of tourists in a bus came by. The scientists poked the tip above the water. Later, the tourists were asked to draw what they had seen in the water. Many of them drew monster-shaped heads.

One strange, but **precise** explanation for the 1930s Nessie sightings comes from Scottish scientist Neil Clark. Clark discovered that traveling circuses during that time would let their animals rest on the banks of Loch Ness. These animals included elephants.

The elephants would cool off in the water. When seen from the surface, the trunk of an elephant could look like a dinosaur's long neck. The elephant's head and back might look like a dinosaur's humps.

Some Nessie sightings have turned out to be nothing more than hoaxes, or fakes. Decades after Robert Wilson snapped his famous photo, the truth came out. The picture was fake. The sea monster's

head had been created from plastic. It was stuck onto a cheap toy submarine. The fake was floated in the water for the photo.

Bigfoot

Another famous monster is North America's Bigfoot. This mysterious monster is supposed to be the missing link between humans and apes. Stories about Bigfoot have been around for decades.

In the stories, people went walking in the wilderness. Suddenly, from nowhere, out popped the beast—huge, furry, smelly, and scary. The Bigfoot tales matched up with old Native American legends about creatures that roamed the woods. In the 1920s, this creature was given the name Sasquatch.

The Sasquatch-Bigfoot story really took off in 1958. That year, a California tree cutter named Ray Wallace claimed to have made a discovery. In the ground near a logging camp, he found a pair of 16-inch-long footprints. The footprints didn't belong to any known animal. They looked almost human, but they were much, much bigger!

Newspapers ran stories about Wallace's find. Soon there was a relentless increase in Bigfoot sightings. Reports came in from California, Canada, and the Pacific Northwest.

The biggest event for Bigfoot believers came in 1967. That year, a rodeo cowboy and Bigfoot hunter named Roger Patterson headed up into a mountain valley at Six Rivers National Forest in Bluff Creek, California. He had a film camera with him and made a short movie. It showed a giant, apelike creature walking into the woods. The film sparked even more interest in the monster.

A plaster cast of a Bigfoot tracks

One of the people who saw the film was Dr. Jeffrey Meldrum. Meldrum was just a child when he saw the film, but he stayed interested in Bigfoot as he grew up. His interest led to him studying sciences in college, which he hoped he could use to prove the existence of Bigfoot. Today, Meldrum is a professor at Idaho State University. Like most teachers, he gives **lectures** on anatomy and works in a laboratory, but he also researches and has become an expert on Bigfoot.

Meldrum's laboratory is full of normal glass **beakers** and **microscopes**. But it also contains 200 plaster casts. These are molds made from Bigfoot tracks people claim to have found. Meldrum thinks these prints are the best evidence that Bigfoot is real. Whenever he gets a chance, he's out in the wild trying to track down more prints.

Meldrum, however, is almost alone among scientists. Most think there's little reason to believe oversized ape-men are living in North America. As with Nessie, scientists think the explanation for most Bigfoot sightings is simple. People see what they want to see. If people are looking for Bigfoot, their minds are ready to see ape-men in place of deer or bears.

People in Canada's Yukon Territory were sure they had seen a Bigfoot. They had spotted giant hairy animals outside their homes. They even found clumps of the Bigfoot's hair. The hair was sent to Dr. David Coltman's laboratory. He looked at it under a microscope and identified it. The hair didn't belong to a Bigfoot. It came from a bison, the ordinary American buffalo.

As with Nessie, some Bigfoot sightings are probably fakes. Two researchers looked at the Patterson film. They stopped it in places to look at it closely.

At one place in the film, the researchers saw metal clips on the beast. Most likely, these clips were part of an ape costume. Others researchers studied Patterson's life. It seems he wanted to make money from Bigfoot even before he went into Six Rivers forest. It turns out he had made other, clearly fake, Bigfoot films. The Wallace footprints from 1958 also turned out to be hoax. After Ray Wallace died in 2002, his children spilled the secret.

"It was just a joke," said his son Michael. Ray loved playing pranks. He made the prints himself using fake wooden feet.

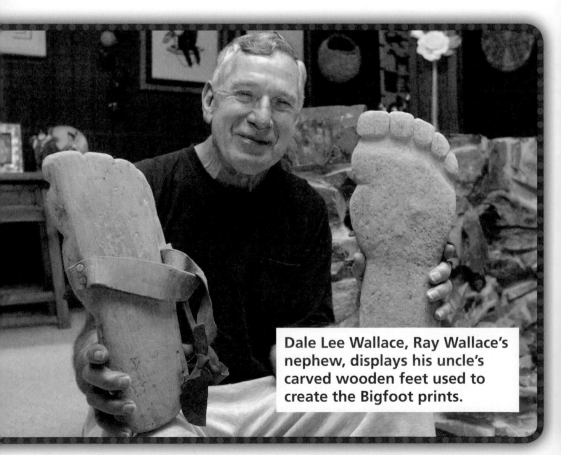

Dale Lee Wallace, Ray Wallace's nephew, displays his uncle's carved wooden feet used to create the Bigfoot prints.

Tom Biscardi

Still, news about Bigfoot keeps coming. In August 2008, Tom Biscardi, a man who runs a Bigfoot Web site, made an incredible announcement. A Bigfoot hadn't just been seen. A Bigfoot had been found! Two Bigfoot hunters had discovered the body of a "very frightening" dead Bigfoot in Northern Georgia. They dragged the body out of the woods. According to the hunters, there were even more Bigfoot bodies back in the forest.

Biscardi said he was "150 percent" sure the Bigfoot body was real. The hunters were going to take the body into a laboratory. They would look at its cells under a microscope. They would prove that the body was real.

Biscardi believed the hunters. He paid them lots of money to have the frozen Bigfoot body shipped to him. When it arrived, Biscardi was crushed. The frozen Bigfoot was just a rubber Gorilla suit disguised with animal body parts. Nobody has come forward with any true evidence of Bigfoot's body to this day.

The Abominable Snowman

Like North America and Scotland, Asia has its own mysterious monster. It's called the Abominable Snowman, or the Yeti. As for Nessie and Bigfoot, there are photos and sketches supposedly showing the monster. This mythical beast is half-ape, half-man, just like Bigfoot. Also like Bigfoot, the Yeti is hairy and tall.

Stories about the snowman come from India, China, Tibet, Nepal, and even Russia. The beast is usually seen in the snow-covered Himalayas, the tallest mountains on Earth. As with Bigfoot, many people claimed that they found oversized Yeti tracks in the snow.

When Edmund Hillary became one of the first people to climb Mount Everest in 1953, he heard tales about the Yeti. About ten years later, Hillary went back on a special trip just to look for one.

Hillary's team went to an area of the Himalayas where people had seen huge Yeti tracks. They brought all kinds of gear, including microphones and cameras.

They hoped to record the Yeti's high-pitched screams with the microphones and the Yeti's movements with cameras. The cameras were attached to trip wires. If the Yeti tripped over a wire, the camera would start filming. But even with all the equipment, Hillary never saw the Yeti.

Hillary didn't come back with an explanation for the Yeti tracks. He decided they came from other animals, such as snow leopards, bears, wolves, or even from humans. When mountain sun shined down on the tracks, they would melt, which made them look bigger. Human footprints could become nearly two feet long. Footprints this big could easily be mistaken for those of a monster.

Sir Edmund Hillary and his expedition team

People still claim to see Abominable Snowmen in the Himalayas. In 2008, a forester in India said he had seen a Yeti walking for three days in a row. He even collected hairs from the creature.

Scientists in Britain examined the hairs under microscopes. At first they were excited. They couldn't match the hair with any known animal. Soon, however, the hairs were studied further, and scientists in the United States identified them. The hairs didn't come from an ape-man, but from an uncommon mountain goat!

The Yeti hairs really came from the Goral goat.

A supposed Chupacabra sighting

Other Monsters

Nessie, Bigfoot, and Yeti aren't the world's only mysterious monsters. Canadians have Ogopogo, a Nessielike monster with flippers and a horselike head. Believers say that Ogopogo swims around a large lake in British Columbia.

Chupacabra is another monster. Stories about this legendary creature are told in Puerto Rico, Mexico, and all over South America. The Chupacabra is kind of a cross between a fox and a vampire bat, with green skin and long fangs. It is blamed for attacking animals, often goats, and killing them by sucking their blood.

The Chupacabra doesn't sound much like the other monsters. It does, however, have one thing in common with them. Like Bigfoot, Nessie, and the Yeti, no Chupacabra has ever been caught. Perhaps people who claim to have seen a Chupacabra have actually seen dogs or coyotes.

So if none of these monsters are real, why have so many people reported seeing them? Some of them are jokers like Ray Wallace. They like to have a little fun. Some hope to make money with their hoaxes.

Others are simply mistaken. The fact is, you can't always believe your eyes. A bear can look like an ape-man when it's running through the trees. In addition, it's fun to believe that monsters can be real.

T-shirt from Loch Ness

Giant squid

Sometimes, stories about monsters do turn out to be true. In the 19th century, sailors told tales of sea monsters. These animals had very long arms that looked strong enough to grab a ship or a whale. Unlike other scary monster stories, this one turned out to be true. In time, scientists identified these monsters as giant squids, the true monsters of the sea. Scientists think they can grow to be 50 to 75 feet long!

Once in a while, these huge animals wash up on shore or get caught in a fishing net. They are always dead, however. For decades, scientists tried to find a living one without any luck. Then in 2005, a Japanese crew finally did it. Using underwater cameras, they captured a giant squid on film. For once, a mysterious monster was shown to be real.

Glossary

analysis *n.* a method of studying a thing or determining its essential features

beakers *n.* thin, flat-bottomed glass cups with no handles, used in laboratories

hollow *adj.* having nothing inside

identify *v.* recognize

lectures *n.* planned speeches or talks, usually for the purpose of instruction

microscopes *n.* tools with lenses for magnifying very small things

precise *adj.* very exact or accurate

relentless *adj.* without pity; harsh

Reader Response

1. Look over the information about Nessie and the Yeti. How are they similar? How are they different? Use a Venn Diagram like the one below to organize information for your answer.

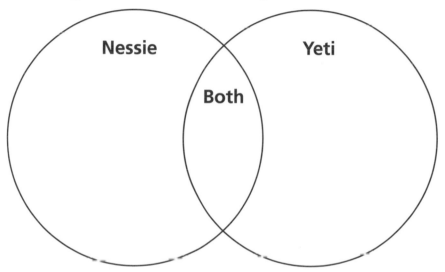

Nessie   Yeti

Both

2. Reread pages 7 and 8. What did you visualize as you read these pages? How does visualizing this help you understand the scientists in the book and better understand what you read?

3. How would you use the word *precise* in the context of a laboratory? Use the word in a sentence.

4. Which of the monsters described in this book would you like to see or know more about? Why?

Social Studies

Genre	Comprehension Skills and Strategy	Text Features
Nonfiction	• Compare and Contrast • Fact and Opinion • Visualize	• Captions • Headings • Map • Glossary

Scott Foresman Reading Street 4.4.1

Scott Foresman
is an imprint of

ISBN-13: 978-0-328-51657-5
ISBN-10:   0-328-51657-0

To the Moon!

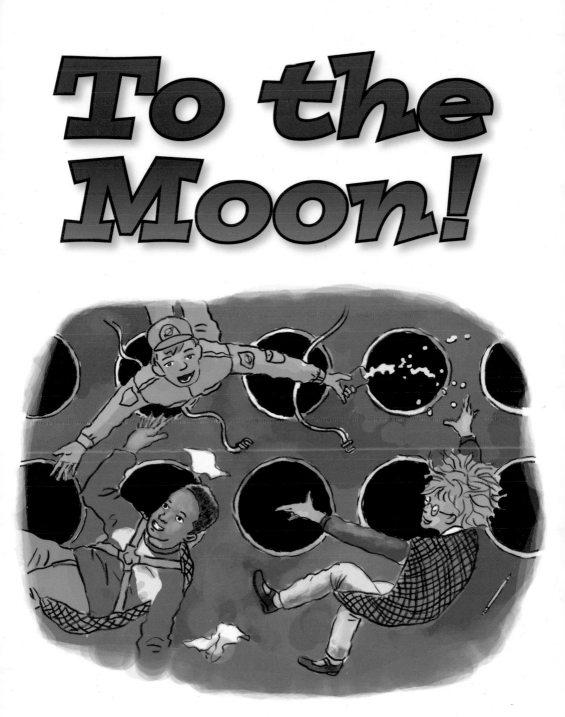

by Jesse McDermott
illustrated by Victor Kennedy

Vocabulary

loomed

rille

runt

staggered

summoning

taunted

trench

trudged

Word count: 1,767

Note: The total word count includes words in the running text and headings only. Numerals and words in chapter titles, captions, labels, diagrams, charts, graphs, sidebars, and extra features are not included.